Live the Internet Life

Chapter 1

Internet Times

We live in very exciting times where the Internet affords all of us all manner of opportunities we could not even imagine were possible a mere decade and a half back. To the Internet generation names like Google, eBay, Microsoft Outlook, AOL Instant Messenger, Amazon, and lately Facebook, and Twitter are a part of their social consciousness much like newspapers, radio and TV were to the earlier generation.

The biggest gift of the Internet is that it liberates you to be what you want to be. You want to be a rock star, for practically no cost at all you can create music upload it on the Internet and reach it to a vast audience.

Whatever may be your dream, the Internet can enable it. Sites like Facebook which reach hundreds of millions of people give you the wherewithal to get your message across to vast numbers of people in real time.

Something like this would require millions of dollars advertising and publicity costs in addition to the cost of production. You on the other hand do not require to hunt for record labels, financiers or publicity agents. All you need is a laptop with Internet connectivity. The great thing about the Internet is that it can make you famous irrespective of your social and economic background.

You don't need sugar daddies or mentors to get there. You have something to say; there will be an audience out there to hear it. The Internet lets you reach them without any encumbrances.

This book points out the way to youngsters who want to use the Internet to harness their potential but are not quite sure how to go about it. It explains the nuts and bolts of deploying the immense power of the Internet to their own use in a fun and easy to understand manner.

Chapter 2

Online Celebrity

We have all heard stories about obscure teenagers overnight turning into huge celebrities. Children really, who by the time they came into their teens turned their everyday hobbies and passions into multi-million dollar enterprises; all by reaching out to vast numbers of like-minded individuals on the Internet.

Before we begin to understand what it takes to bring about these tremendous transformations let us begin by going ahead of us and taking a sneak preview into what sort of life-style changes a formerly regular person experiences as a result of him having become an online celebrity.

You become an internet millionaire at a young age; the world is your oyster. The best cars, snazzy mansions, incredible holidays, the best people to date-you will get that and more. If you are really top of the heap every newspaper and magazine worth their salt would like to feature you, and there will be offers to write books (perhaps your autobiography which can be turned into a book).

Large multinational corporations would like to sign business deals with you and you will be e a youth icon and role model for the young of the world.

Successful Online

There are any number of people who have made a mark for themselves by skilfully using the Internet to promote themselves or their business models. You will find that a great many of them started off fairly young sometimes in their teens, and they shared a strong belief in their conviction that they had the right product and service for which there existed a healthy market, and they gave their all in its pursuit.

Not all of them achieve rare and unprecedented growth and there are many many others who may not count among the world's richest folk, but still have grown exceedingly rich and famous by any standards of the world.

Quite honestly the examples are far too numerous, but what is striking is that most of these individuals started with an original idea at a very young age and made their millions while still under 30 years of age. Never in the history of mankind since the advent of civilisation, have so many young people made such prodigious amounts of money at such a young age.

It is the power of the Internet which has given wing to the imagination of these new age entrepreneurs and given them the ability to soar. Truly the invention of the Internet must rank as highly as the invention of the wheel, the electric bulb and the automobile in as much that its impact has been epochal.

What is in it for me?

What can success on the Internet give you? This is a question which has many parts and you may wonder as to what it is that becoming an Internet success holds out for you?

Is it about the money, the fame, the adulation, the popularity, the convergence with likeminded people or is it about notoriety? Well the fact of the matter is that the Internet and Internet millionaires are a recent phenomenon and the jury is yet out on whether it is all good, or whether it is a mixed blessing, and no doubt as the years go by and the golden boys of this era add a few grey hairs to their temples, sociologists and psychologists will write their theses and treatises on the subject; but right now suffice it to say that the Internet provides unprecedented opportunity, but along with it come the pitfalls, which are really part of the territory if you are looking at blazing a trail and making a name for yourself.

Consider this. The Internet is a vast ocean of information which you can harness and put to use to further your own objectives. Now your objective may be something as simple as help in your homework assignment, or you may want to run an online pizza delivery business. You may even want to write your autobiography and reach it to as many people as possible across the globe. The Internet will empower you to go ahead and accomplish this.

It will let you communicate with whoever you want anywhere in the world. This means that you can work and entertain with like-minded people when you want and where you want without being at a disadvantage because of you age, sex nationality, religion or geography.

Now this can be a tremendously liberating thing. You are free to choose who you want to work with at what time and on what terms. The same applies to entertainment.

What this means is that the very paradigm of living life as we know it has changed. For the first time in the history of mankind one has the truest personal freedom of choosing one's career, where you choose your own schedule and give full rein to your creative imagination.

This does not of course mean that there is no flip side. Of course there is, just as there is in everything in life. There is danger of spamming, identity theft, pornography and vicious virus attacks. But these are illegal activities and you should take all measures to protect yourself against them.

If you indulge in such activities yourself, you do so at your own peril as you are breaking the law. Then there are other pitfalls, not the least among them being Internet addiction.

The Internet is a tool that you can use to get ahead in life and also indulge in some harmless entertainment. If you make it the be all and end all of your life, then you will have no life to talk about. Your online friends can never fill in for real, physical contact and interaction.

Neither can online gaming take the place of a game of basket- ball. You have got to put things in perspective and you will be alright. For example take the case of Facebook- a great way to socialise and re-establish contact with long lost friends. But you know what? Don't be the fool who lives to update his or her status on it.

Who wants to know what you had for breakfast today? Try Facebook to launch your business career or finding employment. It lends itself very nicely to such things with its vast reach. The Internet can empower you like nothing else, but you got to be focussed on your goals, and not get side-tracked by its many distractions.

It's like life itself. The choices you make decide where you get. You can use the internet to sell your skills and get rich. If fame is your thing, the Internet gives you access to a vast audience, and if you are up to no good and indulge in dirty tricks and sleaze- well the Internet can provide notoriety too. As they say-to each his own.

Chapter 3

Online Better Than Offline

Most people in the Western world and large sections in the rest of the world have a real life persona and an online persona. This is especially true of young people, also known as the Internet generation. Most people these days communicate by email rather than rely on the good old postal services. Texting and video chatting have become mainstream and e-commerce has willy nilly entered all our lives.

 Don't we remit money or receive it into our bank accounts online, and haven't we all used the credit card to make purchases online. We all swear by e-bay for God's sake! The point that one is trying to make here is that we have a very active online life that co-exists with our offline life.

But a debate really arises when we have to choose between performing the same function in the traditional or offline fashion or the contemporary online way. Take the case of making payments. You have the option of writing a cheque or making an online transfer.

Cheques are relatively safer, but can't match the speed or convenience of an online money transfer. Another example is socialising. Communicating via the net obliterates distance and time differences, but if you want to enjoy a coffee together with your friend or watch the sunset together, you have to do it offline.

But the wonderful thing is that as online technology evolves we may be able to even do things that we right now consider impossible- like smelling coffee! The coming days will see the Online vs Off line debate getting more and more interesting.

What makes online famous a different kettle of fish? Now you might turn around and say that to me it does not matter that I got famous the old fashioned way, without having to use the Internet, and what ultimately matters is the result.

You may be right and you may be wrong. While it is true that one can get famous using traditional media like TV, newspapers and magazines, one cannot claim that these media represent you and what you have comprehensively.

Getting famous using the Internet on the other hand lets your target-audience know you and what you stand for more intimately. They can personally connect on your blog, and you can chat up with them as frequently as you want.

You can use analytical tools that will let you know precisely who is interested in your offering and how many of those are establishing contact. The thing about being spotted on the Internet is that it is a very democratic and a cheap as well as fair process where everybody gets a shot at being successful whereas in the traditional model you need to knows how to work the levers of the system for things to really work for you.

Look at this in another manner. In the old days one relied on one's family, community, society and church to get along in life.

One needed that support. As time went along and technology reduced our dependence on people, one's number of friends and acquaintances dropped dramatically. In the modern era, the time immediately preceding the Internet saw most people having about three people they counted as friends.

This was fine except that you could not use the three to spread the word about, say the new book you wrote. You would have to pay professionals to do that. With the advent of Internet all of that has changed. The average person has more than hundred friends on the various social networking sites and these are a valuable resource in case you want the word spread about something.

 Word can spread like a viral infection on the Internet and make a mega celebrity out of nobody in a matter of two or three days. This even has a term-viral marketing. So you see the Internet has changed the rules of the game completely and the goal posts have been moved a lot closer for everyone's convenience.

Be known online

The online world has assumed a huge amount of significance in today's times and this is only going to grow and grow. It would therefore stand you in very good stead to mark your presence in it, in a very telling way.

You simply have to develop your social presence in a manner that you are effectively able to leverage your attributes, skills, likes and dislikes to a vast and appropriate audience. Social networking sites led by Facebook and Twitter are fast and ruthlessly efficient enablers in this- far more effective than traditional media like newspapers and television, and best of all cheaply available and accessible to everyone.

Today the youth are defining and constantly reshaping and evolving the digital world by their socialising, entertaining, learning and studying and following the latest trends online. You are not a part of it, you are don't exist, (at least not digitally). Period.

In order to be heard you have to be on top of the form. E-mail and Instant Messaging are baby steps in this world. You have to be part of online communities where you contribute actively and constantly interact while at the same time learning to innovate.

Be it blogging, web-casting, trending, on-line trading-your transactions will build up for you an online profile by which people will gauge you. Much like in the world of finance, each country or for that matter each individual has a credit rating, so it is in the world of the Internet. You have to make your presence felt.

The power of the Internet as a harbinger of change was brought home by the highly effective way in which Arab youth were able to harness its power to bring about The Arab spring, the movement that called for reform in the way people were governed.

This was something the previous generations could not achieve, as they did not have the tremendous power of the internet at their disposal. We are in the throes of the mighty digital revolution and the youth are the ones who are driving it and it is in their individual interest to put their individual stamp on it. Uninterrupted economic success

The Internet is a medium that can be effectively used to achieve overnight success. Now whether this success is a flash in the pan or sustainable over a long period of time depends upon how you play the game.

Overnight success does not come to many and the lucky few who get it might have worked really hard to achieve it or might have been plain lucky, but what is important is how they manage it, or whether they are able to sustain it or indeed grow it.

The Internet not only empowers the individual but by extension the community, the nation and finally the world. In countries like India for example with every passing year Internet penetration increases and with it increases the opportunity for the Indian youth who have already gained a formidable reputation for their IT prowess, to make India the crucible of new ideas and innovation.

This has the potential to pitch-fork the Indian nation way ahead of where it is now and quite rapidly and truly become the world's economic power house. India with its democracy, rule of law and well established institutions patterned after those of the West is perhaps better equipped to achieve this than an at present richer, but dictatorial China, which denies its citizens the freedom to think freely and therefore innovate, a prerequisite in this bold new world of the Internet with its ever evolving and changing by the minute paradigm.

Truly living the Internet life will be the ultimate game changer for mankind and we are in the throes of a lifestyle metamorphosis which is of no less significance than the momentous occasion millions of years ago when man first learnt to walk upright. Nothing is going to be the same again.

Chapter 4

Getting famous

The Internet can be used to get famous. Really famous. There are several ways of doing that. Some have been well documented and in the last chapter we discussed the attributes required to get famous. Given below are five unknown, very fun, but highly effective ways of getting famous, leveraging the potential of the Internet.

Videos that go viral

We come across these supposedly accidentally shot videos of someone doing something remarkable without noticing that they are being filmed. The person may be doing summersaults on the roof of a high rise building, practising his flips right next to a sheer 100 foot drop, oblivious to the danger and enjoying his routine. Somebody uploads it and the clip has millions of hits online.

Soon the man's identity is known and he becomes a household name, and the media is at his door with interview requests, and he is even asked to lecture school kids on the benefits of exercise. Sounds far-fetched but this is how the phenomenon of viral videos pans out.

 And mind you these are invariably pre-planned and anything but spontaneous. Now what is noteworthy here is that a viral video can make you very famous in the proverbial overnight time-span, and if you can successfully effect one you have had it made. If one were to learn from the various examples of successful viral videos one will realise that it is not really that difficult to pull it off. One of the ground rules to follow is that the length has to be kept short what with people's short attention spans and the veritable deluge of viral videos that has descended upon us.

It has to be remembered that a video is not inherently viral. It has to be worked upon and made that way. A whopping 3 billion videos are viewed on YouTube every day! How do you make yours viral in such a scenario?

The content needs to be reached to the right target audience first for it to receive the right push that will make it viral. To ensure that the video gets the initial attention it does you of course have to create a good first impression.

Then the description or transcription that accompanies the video is important too and the key words should be chosen with care. Remember that YouTube is also a social medium. So get the conversation flowing back and forth by initiating it and actively participating in it.

Get the traffic flowing so that it eventually it reaches viral proportions. So we see that viral video are a proven and extremely effective way of gaining fame, provided one is able to use it the right way

Go Blog

Blogging is one of the simplest and most effective ways of getting famous, and the best part is that you could be anybody-the average Joe or the wiz-kid of the block; both of you have an equal chance to hit it big by blogging.

The basic premise is that there have to be numerous people who are more or less like you and would respond positively and appreciatively to what you put up on your blog. The way to achieve success is by updating your blog on a regular and consistent basis and by focusing on quality.

It might take some time for you to build up your audience, but you will get there if you persevere. The trick is to socialise. Comment on other people's blogs and get them to comment on yours.

Let people know about your blog but do not overdo it. Use the right vehicles like Facebook and Twitter to reach your message to a vast audience in an unobtrusive way. It might also be a good idea to enable sharing buttons on your website.

That apart, you can share links with other websites. When you do that, traffic gets diverted from your site to the ones that are linked. Those sites will get to know of this through a ping back and they may in turn get interested in yours. This way you create a virtuous cycle.

Putting together a side-bar embellished with link widgets takes you a step further. While it is all very well to be blogging regularly you should monitor the direction that your efforts are taking. Find out what constitutes the major portion of your traffic, and customise your posts to cater for that section.

It also pays to be a bit smart. For instance you can closely study the strategy applied by the most successful bloggers and try and replicate it. It might work wonderfully for you and in double quick time too. Another way of getting noticed by the right people is to occasionally blog as guest on other sites which have synergy with your blog.

This will put you in direct contact with just the target audience you have always drooled over. This will be your chance to win them over. In essence blogging is something where time is on your side and you can and will willy nilly make a great success of your blog, if that is what you want to do. Really, this is one of the best ways to get famous.

The truth of this is borne out by the many success stories of bloggers who have become celebrities in their own right by the very power of their blog posts. The most famous blog in the world is the Huffington post, which specialises in breaking news pertaining to a wide array of subjects-world news, entertainment, business, politics and fashion.

You have traffic; the biggies will be waiting in the wings to pay you a huge some for your coveted blog. That is the way the cookie usually crumbles if you can show substantial traffic to your site.

If you can showcase the tremendous power of a blog in terms of how famous it can make you and the kind of revenue you can possibly generate. Now not everyone will possibly be this successful, but one can understand that a fair degree of success is possible for anyone who is able to follow the methodologies discussed above.

The degree of success of course depends upon the level of innovation and capacity to leverage displayed by the individual. Nothing like Entertaining If there is anything that people take to instantly, be it the offline world or online world it has to be entertainment. Music, dance, food, fashion and culture make the world go. And if you can put up stuff online that people find genuinely entertaining you are set to achieve success, fame and wealth.

If you are a comedian or a singer or perhaps a painter there is no better way of acquiring a fan base, than being on the Internet. People have this urge to know the smallest detail about famous entertainer-their hobbies, their food habits, their hang out joints and what it is that they wear.

If you can get a sizeable group of people genuinely interested in your craft, you will have them eating out of your hand, by leveraging such information on the Internet. Get across to your target audience by writing blogs about your performances and posting videos.

Give them a glimpse into your life. Your joint performances with other artists, any new deals you may have signed-the works. You have got to remember that your success and livelihood depends upon your fans being happy.

So take full advantage of this interactive platform and get to know your fans up close and personally. Respond to their comments and criticism, chat with them online, send those mails, do everything it takes to keep them hooked on to you and see where that gets you.

The thing that is of paramount importance for you should be of identifying the right niche and segment that you want to focus your energies on. If for example you are excellent at rock ballads but can sing hip hop too, rather than diluting your image by catering to both the segments, it would make sense to focus on your core competency.

You will naturally attract more and better quality traffic with something you are really good at rather than in dabbling in several things you are only average at. In economics this is referred to as the theory of the comparative cost advantage.

Once you are sure of your genre, you have got to give it your all. Use blogging, social media and YouTube for all its worth and try and form associations everywhere. A multi-pronged online approach will create opportunities which will sometimes exceed your wildest expectations.

A singer might be approached by a multinational record label and a cookery blogger might get approached by a TV company for his own show. The online world has so many examples of people fulfilling dreams of a lifetime simply by being on the Internet.

The point to be noted is that notoriety is the flip side of fame and many people leverage it on the Internet. As long as you get the traffic and don't break any laws, you will be attractive to marketers who will want to be a part of the action.

You think you have what it takes to become an entertainer make the Internet your friend. It is cheap, easily accessible and can put you in instant touch with your prospective audience. Plus you get real time feedback on your performance, which you can effectively use to improve your performance and make it more in line with what people want. If you get it right, in time you are bound to grow big.

Be a specialist

The Internet is a world that is teeming with people's posts, blogs, articles, pictures, videos, e-books, games and some not so savoury content. How do you get noticed in this bewildering maze of content?

Going back to the economic theory of the advantages of comparative cost, by specialising in a particular niche. Now what can that niche be? It is something that you are particularly good at. Something that you can call your own.

You are so good and adept at providing that product and service there is no one else who can replace you. The online world is driven by content or information. If you are effectively meeting specific requirements of a set of people better than anyone else be it in the shape of music that your produce or game that you create, then for that particular niche you are irreplaceable.

The fact of the matter is that your target audience expects you to be an expert. So you had better be, by doing research and refining your skills. Make it your niche and yours alone and nobody else's. Once you have the above sorted out and have traffic in place you can go ahead and make money from this traffic.

This can be done by signing up for an affiliate program that lets advertisers place their advertisements on your site for a consideration. Not only do you make money by marketing the product or service you specialise in, you also leverage the traffic to your site to earn more money-a win-win situation for you.

You can learn from the examples of others who have done wonderfully well for themselves by focusing on the right niche. You would be surprised that some of the best examples of niche marketing are not small timers but large corporations.

Be Special

Following up on the above where one talked about creating or discovering one's own niche; this cannot and will not happen unless your product or service is unique and in a class of its own. Before you come to as to what makes you or your offering unique, we need to address a more basic question. Who are the people that you plan to serve?

For example if you plan to be an author, you cannot be writing about everything under the sun and expect to make any headway. There would be so many like you who wouldn't have the slightest clue about what the profile of their average reader would be.

However if you want to be known as an author who writes books whose characters hail from Brisbane, you would be able to identify your target audience-the people of Brisbane. Now you can go all out and woo the people of Brisbane. How many authors would there all of whose characters would be from Brisbane?

That would make you unique. You would be able to through you books on the city explore different facets of it. -its history, its people, its culture, its cuisine, its entertainment hot-spots and so on. You could literally go to town with snippets from your forthcoming books, information about the real life people and events that inspired you, the part of Brisbane you grew up in and other like trivia. By and by you would create a unique position as the definitive voice on Brisbane.

If you are looking for examples of uniqueness saving the day for websites, the successful ones are all unique. Take the case of Facebook which propounded a unique model of online social networking.

Today there may be many copycat sites. But can they replicate even a tiny fraction of the success that accrued to it? Not a chance! Because they were clearly not unique.

Well Facebook may be a legendary example, but there are many many more which validate the contention that being unique is the first step taken towards online celebrity and fame. Some even go the over the top and eccentric way to prove that they are unique, but when the stakes are high can it be otherwise? Work out your uniqueness quotient before you even begin to think of making mass contact.

That being said, there is nothing in this world that stops you from finding your niche. The Internet universe is a much fairer and more democratic organism than what has ever evolved over the eons, and everybody has a fair chance at communicating with like-minded individuals. This is the Internet's greatest strength. Make it yours.